The Wounded Spirit

Unpacking and Unpeeling Life's Hurts for Healing

A Companion Workbook
For Personal or Group Use

The Wounded Spirit

Unpacking and Unpeeling Life's Hurts for Healing

A Companion Workbook For Personal or Group Use

By
Frank R. Shivers

LIGHTNING SOURCE
1246 Heil Quaker Blvd.
La Vergne, TN

Library of Congress Cataloging-in-Publication Data

Shivers, Frank R., 1949-
The Wounded Spirit, Companion Workbook / Frank Shivers
ISBN 978-1-878127-24-2

Library of Congress Control Number:
2015911564

Cover design by
Tim King of Click Graphics, Inc.

For Information:
Frank Shivers Evangelistic Association
P. O. Box 9991
Columbia, South Carolina 29290
www.frankshivers.com

God is bigger than your problems. Whatever worries press upon you today, put them in God's hands and leave them there.[1]—Billy Graham

What's a crushed spirit? A crushed spirit then is to look out at life and to have no desire for it, have little or no joy in it, have no passion to get out there and deal with it. Of course, there are degrees of a crushed spirit. It can be anywhere from listlessness and restlessness to discouragement to despondency to being very, very cast down and to losing all desire to live.[2]—Tim Keller

---

[1] *Promises and Prayers for a Cherished Friend,* 176.

[2] Keller.

Contents

About This Workbook

This workbook is designed to be used in personal or group settings in studying *The Wounded Spirit*. It is a supplement to the book, not a standalone resource. Each chapter has three learning/teaching sections: **Review**—*Truths the Chapter Taught* (essence of the chapter); **Reflect**—*Consider What This Means* (personal expression of the deeper meaning drawn from the chapter); and **Respond**—*What Will You Do with What You Know?* (application to your life).

The fact that you purchased the book and workbook indicates that you are a victim of a wounded spirit and desire healing. It is my heartfelt prayer that as you undertake this study, the Holy Spirit will "sift" all that is written to make it applicable and thus greatly beneficial to your life.

1

The Wounded Spirit

Spirit wounding may be defined as a crushing and bruising injury to the soul. "We should be more careful not to wound a brother's spirit than we are to refrain from doing a bodily injury. The latter may be healed by medical applications; the former is more severe in its effects and is often irremediable."[3]

Review—*Truths the Chapter Taught*

(1) What is meant by the term "wounded spirit?"

_____

_____

(2) Medical personnel talk of "weeping wounds," wounds which continue to fester, discharge and ooze, refusing to heal due to noxious matter. Contrast such wounds with the wounding of the spirit (book Preface).

_____

_____

(3) How do we get our spirit wounded?

_____

_____

(4) Why is this subject an important issue?

_____

_____

(5) Signs of a wounded spirit include diminishing of mental, spiritual and emotional stamina, lashing out, bitterness, blaming God, paralyzing guilt, cutting remarks, withdrawal from others, and diminished hopes. Name four more signs.

_____

_____

---

[3] Spence-Jones, 350.

(6) What does a person's sensitivity level have to do with some cases of spirit wounding?

_____

_____

(7) Identify various forms of spirit wounding? Betrayal, slander,

_____

_____

(8) According to C. H. Spurgeon why is the best cure for a wounded spirit its prevention?

_____

_____

(9) Stated are ten preventatives of a wounded spirit. Define each.

(A) Be a follower of Christ.

_____

_____

(B) Pursue Christian maturity.

_____

_____

(C) Apply God's Word

_____

_____

(D) Consider the source.

_____

_____

(E) Prayer

_____

_____

The Wounded Spirit

(F) Clarify for understanding.

_____

_____

(G) Don't rate human opinion too highly.

_____

_____

(H) Don't be overly sensitive.

_____

_____

(I) Rely upon Jesus.

_____

_____

(J) Make sure you embrace rational not irrational beliefs.

_____

_____

(10) What heart wounds are inescapable? Bereavement,

_____

_____

(11) What is the contrast between physical and spirit wounding?

_____

_____

Reflect—*Consider What This Means*

(1) Write out an experience of spirit wounding that either you or another experienced. Share its type, cause and hurt.

_____

_____

(2) John Stott states, "Although we have responsibilities to others, we are primarily accountable to God. It is before Him that we stand, and to Him that one day we must give an account. We should not therefore rate human opinion too highly, becoming depressed when criticized and elated when flattered."[4] Explain how some spirit wounding may be avoided by practicing Stott's counsel.

_____

_____

(3) "Thou wilt keep him in perfect peace, whose mind is stayed on thee: because he trusteth in thee" (Isaiah 26:3). God promises perfect peace to His children, but it is conditional. State the two conditions of Isaiah 26:3 and their apparent meanings (include ways the condition may be fully realized).

_____

_____

Respond—*What Will You Do with What You Know?*

(1) In the *Review—Truths the Chapter Taught* section, you indicated the eight preventatives of a wounded spirit. Which three especially need to be applied to your life and why?

_____

_____

_____

(2) What role may you play in prevention of spirit wounding to another?

_____

_____

_____

(3) Describe your sensitivity level to criticism and venomous talk addressed at you.

_____

---

[4] Stott.

The Wounded Spirit

Based upon your sensitivity level, what might you do to avoid being wounded?

_____

_____

2
Wounded by Betrayal

"He who covers and forgives an offense seeks love, but he who repeats or harps on a matter separates even close friends" (Proverbs 17:9, Amplified Bible). "It is a terrible wounding," states C. H. Spurgeon, "when he who should have been your friend becomes your foe and when, like your Lord, you also have your Judas Iscariot. It is not easy to bear misrepresentation and falsehood, to have your purest motives misjudged. This is a very painful kind of wounded spirit." [5]

Review—*Truths the Chapter Taught*

(1) Complete the following sentence. To be betrayed means "to disclose a secret or confidence treacherously; to _____, or be disloyal to a person's _____; to disappoint the _____ of."

(2) How else might you define betrayal?

_____

_____

(3) Betrayal comes in many forms. List four.

_____

_____

(4) What lesson does Jesus cite in Matthew 24:10?

_____

_____

(5) The Bible records the betrayals of Nehemiah, Samson, Uriah, David, and Jesus. What lesson may be drawn from their betrayals that is applicable to you?

_____

_____

(6) List four reasons for betrayal.

_____

_____

---

[5] Spurgeon, "The Cause and Cure of a Wounded Spirit."

The Wounded Spirit Workbook

Reflect—*Consider What This Means*

(1) Judas' betrayal of Jesus certainly did not hinder God's sovereign plan. What does this truth reveal about betrayal?

_____

(2) Paul cautions, "Never take your own revenge, beloved, but leave room for the wrath of God, for it is written, 'VENGEANCE IS MINE, I WILL REPAY,' says the Lord" (Romans 12:9, NASB). State the meaning of this verse.

_____

_____

(3) Forgive the betrayer and move on with your life. In the Lord's Prayer, Jesus gave instruction to pray in this fashion, "And forgive us our debts, as we forgive our debtors" (Matthew 6:12). The _____ within you will enable (supernatural power) this forgiveness, if you are living under His control.

(4) Cite your reflection of the meaning of the statement: "Sometimes you have to move on without certain people; if they're meant to be in your life, they will catch up."

_____

_____

Respond—*What Will You Do with What You Know?*

(1) Describe an experience of betrayal you have experienced.

_____

_____

(2) Commit yourself to implementing the ten helps stated when faced with betrayal.

(3) What is the primary, pivotal response to betrayal, according to Jesus?

_____

_____

(4) Is there someone to whom you should go expressing sorrow for an act of betrayal against him?

Wounded by Betrayal

If so, ask God for strength to take that step this week.

(5) It's high time to let go of the bitterness and anger toward those who have betrayed you. Right now ask God to forgive you for withholding forgiveness toward the person(s) and take steps for reconciliation. Who is the person you need to contact this week in this regard? _____

3

Wounded by Slander

"An hypocrite with his mouth destroyeth his neighbour" (Proverbs 11:9). "To judge another," states William Barclay, "is to take to ourselves a right to do what God alone has the right to do; and he is a reckless man who deliberately infringes the prerogatives of God. We might think that to speak evil of our neighbor is not a very serious sin. But Scripture would say that it is one of the worst of all because it is a breach of the royal law and an infringement of the rights of God."[6]

Review—*Truths the Chapter Taught*

(1) Who is a slanderer? _____

(2) C. H. Spurgeon calls slander, falsehood, insinuation, ridicule poisoned arrows. In what ways are the foursome poisoned arrows?

_____

_____

(3) Exodus 23:1 and James 4:11 expressly speak against slander. Summarize what each text states in regard to slander.

Exodus 23:1 _____

James 4:11 _____

(4) D. L. Moody depicted slander as "_____ _____."

(5) From whom did slander originate? _____

(6) Slander is highly destructive. Share its destructive power as revealed in the following texts.

Proverbs 16:28; 17:9 _____

Proverbs 18:8; 26:22 _____

Proverbs 16:9 _____

Proverbs 26:20 _____

---

[6] Barclay, *The Daily Study Bible Series,* 112.

(7) Matthew 26:59 details the slandering of Jesus. In what specific manner was Jesus slandered, and what was the result of it?

_____

_____

Reflect—*Consider What This Means*

(1) In Matthew 5:44a, Jesus says, "But I say unto you, Love your enemies, bless them that curse you, do good to them that hate you...." Describe the kind of love Jesus is mandating we have for our enemies.

_____

(2) "....pray for them which despitefully use you, and persecute you" (Matthew 5:44b). The word "despitefully" is the Greek word *epereazo,* which means

_____

_____

(3) What was David's response to slander? (Psalm 7:6–9; 119:23–24)

_____

_____

(4) Joseph was slandered by Mrs. Potiphar. In what ways did God vindicate him?

_____

_____

(5) What is meant by the following statement: "When a mule kicks you, don't let it bother you. Just consider the source"?[7]

_____

_____

---

[7] Swindoll, *Elijah,* 113–114.

Wounded by Slander

Respond—*What Will You Do with What You Know?*

(1) Your first response to slander should be to ask God to help you. Right now spend some quiet moments alone with God pleading for His divine intervention. You may find it helpful to base your prayer upon that of David (Psalm 7:6–9).

(2) Chuck Swindoll offers timely counsel to those who are spreading rumors, lies, and slander against another. He states, "There is nothing more treacherous you could be doing than that. Nothing! If you claim to be a follower of Christ, that must stop. Now! You hurt the body. You disease the church. You ruin the testimony of Christ. There is nothing the lost world loves to hear and see more than the family of God fighting each other."[8] If guilty of slander, ask God's pardon and lay your tongue on the altar of consecration to Him.

(3) Upon being slandered, what should be your response?

_____

_____

(4) "If a man blows out the candle of a Christian's reputation," states C. H. Spurgeon, "God will light it again. If He does not do so in this life, remember that at the resurrection there will be a resurrection of reputations as well as bodies: 'Then shall the righteous shine forth as the sun in the kingdom of their Father.'"[9] What does this statement reveal about vindication from slander?

_____

_____

(5) In *The Imitation of Christ*, Thomas à Kempis states, "Do not let your peace depend on the words of men." How will you apply his words to your present circumstance?

_____

_____

---

[8] Swindoll, *Job*, 180.

[9] Allen, 450.

(6) To whom might you tactfully and graciously speak this week regarding his slandering tongue?

_____

4

Wounded by Bitterness

"Follow peace with all men, and holiness, without which no man shall see the Lord: Looking diligently lest any man fail of the grace of God; lest any root of bitterness springing up trouble you, and thereby many be defiled" (Hebrews 12:14–15). James Merritt said, "Bitterness is harbored hurt hidden in the heart."[10] "The seed of bitterness," states Adrian Rogers, "is a hurt that is planted in someone. It may be intentional or unintentional."[11]

Review—*Truths the Chapter Taught*

(1) Define bitterness. _____

(2) What is the *root* of bitterness?

_____

_____

(3) The *soil* of bitterness is the heart that bears.

_____

_____

(4) Adrian Rogers states that bitterness will affect you physically,

_____ and _____.

(5) Describe King Saul's bitterness toward David (1 Samuel 18:8–9).

_____

_____

(6) There are three forms of bitterness. You may be bitter toward God ("Why did He allow the tragedy to happen?" or "Why didn't He answer my prayer?"); others ("What they did to me is unconscionable, and I will never forgive them." or "I deserved the recognition more than he did.") and _____.

---

[10] Merritt, "Don't Get Bitter; Get Better."

[11] Rogers, "The Root of Bitterness."

(7) Summarize the traits of a bitter person.

_____

_____

_____

Reflect—*Consider What This Means*

(1) Luke 15:27–30 cites the prodigal son's *cold* reception by his brother. What lesson is to be gleaned from the text about the fruits of bitterness?

_____

_____

(2) James states that bitterness is like roots deep in the sod. Contrast the roots of a gigantic tree with the roots of bitterness.

_____

_____

(3) Why was Hannah bitter and at whom?

_____

_____

How did she handle her bitterness?

_____

_____

Respond—*What Will You Do with What You Know?*

(1) How might you know if you are embittered? Check all that apply to you.

_____ I am hostile to a certain person.

_____ I feel good and get great satisfaction when I criticize the person who hurt me.

_____ I endeavor to get others to hold my critical view of the person and get angry when they will not.

Wounded by Bitterness

___ I am determined to get even with the person.

___ Family and friends no longer like my company (some).

___ People avoid me.

___ I boil with rage over the person's elevation, promotion or good fortune.

___ I manifest an "I deserve it more than they do" and "I am better than they are" attitude.

___ I know of my angry disposition but am unwilling to change.

___ My life's purpose is to make the person miserable. They will not get away with hurting me.

___ I know what the Bible says about holding grudges, but I can't let this go.

If you checked any of the statements, you have a problem with bitterness; the more checked, the more serious is the problem.

(2) Joseph was placed in a desert pit by his embittered brothers to die a painful death through starvation. Callously these brothers sat down near the pit to eat while Joseph was "in anguish of his soul," crying out for rescue (Genesis 42:21). If you were Joseph, how might you have reacted to all the hurt at the hands of family that he experienced?

_____

_____

(3) What is the root cause of the bitterness you now embrace?

_____

_____

(4) Being totally frank, have the roots of bitterness toward others escalated? _____

(5) Upon renewing the mind (getting rid of the rotten seeds of bitterness, resentment, anger, etc., through confession) and changing the way you think (regular intake of Scripture privately and corporately, fervent prayer, resolving to think as Christ thinks and act as He would act), you will spiritually, emotionally and perhaps physically (bitterness may contribute to physical ailments) take on a "new shape and figure."

Pause now before the Lord, inviting Him to renew your mind toward them against which you are embittered. Confess the sin of bitterness and claim the blood of Jesus to make you clean every whit from it (1 John 1:7–10).

(6) To remove the injurious poison of bitterness from the soul, it must be dug up by its deepest roots, which will demand the grace and strength of God. It involves not only the Lord's forgiveness but that of the person to whom it is directed (Ephesians 4:32). To what person(s) do you need to confess this sin and ask forgiveness? _____

Plan to make contact with that person this week.

(7) Embittered people are easily spotted. What might you do to help resolve their bitterness?

_____

(8) Memorize Hebrews 12:15 this week.

5

Wounded by Harsh Words of a Friend

"Careless words stab like a sword" (Proverbs 12:18, NCB). "An insincere and evil friend is more to be feared than a wild beast; a wild beast may wound your body, but an evil friend will wound your mind."

Review—*Truths the Chapter Taught*

(1) Encapsulate in a sentence the teaching about the tongue in the following passages:

Proverbs 15:1 _____

Proverbs 12:18 _____

James 3:6 _____

Proverbs 17:14 _____

(2) Describe the "ding-dong" principle of forgiveness.

_____

_____

_____

(3) Chuck Swindoll states that sharp (harsh) words are "like _____; they get embedded in the brain."[12]

(4) Elaborate on the statement: Often it's not what is said that cuts but the manner in which it is spoken.

_____

_____

(5) What is the possible result of harsh, venomous talk toward another? (James 5:3–8)

_____

_____

---

[12] Swindoll, *Paul,* 173.

Reflect—*Consider What This Means*

(1) In Psalm 52:2, David likens the tongue to a "sharp razor." In what ways is the tongue like a "sharp razor"?

_____

_____

(2) It's not a sign of spiritual immaturity to be hurt by venomous words. Why not?

_____

_____

(3) Is there a time when harsh words are permissible/necessary?_____

If so, biblically when and to whom are they sanctioned?

_____

_____

Respond—*What Will You Do with What You Know?*

(1) If injured by a "harsh" tongue, do as Corrie ten Boom did with the German prison keeper; forgive and press on. The longer your hands are on the rope of ill-will, the more difficult it will become to forgive. Take your hands off the rope today by forgiving the person.

(2) What truth was learned regarding your manner of talk to others?

_____

_____

(3) Are you prone to use harsh words or an angry tone when upset by the actions of another? _____

Determine to change with God's help. It may prove helpful to have an accountability partner to confront you when harsh words are used.

(4) Have you injured someone intentionally or unintentionally by sharp words? _____

Resolve this week to seek his forgiveness.

6

Wounded by Disagreement

"Let us therefore make every effort to do what leads to peace and to mutual edification" (Romans 14:19, NIV). Joseph Parker stated, "The holiest men may have ruffled tempers sometimes."[13]

Review—*Truths the Chapter Taught*

(1) What was the reason for the dissension between Paul and Barnabas?

_____

_____

(2) Which of the two was in the right and why?

_____

_____

(3) The real question however is not "Who was right?" but _____
_____. Why do you believe it was or was not right?

_____

_____

(4) What resulted from the contention between these two spiritual giants?

_____

_____

(5) Matthew Henry makes a great observation regarding the separation of Paul and Barnabas. Summarize what he stated.

_____

_____

(6) State the lesson taught in the following texts.

        Galatians 5:15 _____

---

[13] Exell, 452.

Romans 14:19 _____

Philippians 2:3 _____

Proverbs 25:8 _____

(7) In what ways did God bring good from the bad (the contention and separtion between Paul and Barnabas)?

_____

(8) In times of regrettable conflict, it is most important not to allow God's _____ to suffer.

Reflect—*Consider What This Means*

(1) Chuck Swindoll observes, "Paul and Barnabas could have offered a reasonable compromise. Giving in would not have meant heresy."[14] Share some possible *compromises* that these men may have made to avoid the conflict and separation.

_____

_____

_____

_____

(2) In 1 Samuel 23, King Saul is in hot pursuit of David for the kill. Just as Saul is about to make the capture, he is pulled away miraculously to fight the Philistines. David is spared. But in 1 Samuel 24, we learn that when the Philistines were dealt a blow, Saul returned to pursue David. What spiritual lesson may be gleaned from Saul's determination to kill David?

_____

_____

_____

(3) Relationships may be irrevocably impacted due to a *sudden* dispute. Do you know of an instant when such occurred, and if so, elaborate?

_____

[14] Swindoll, *Paul,* 177.

Wounded by Disagreement

_____

_____

_____

(4) What is the meaning of the following two statements? Even though Barnabas and Paul never reunited, we have reason to believe they were reconciled. Reconciliation may occur without reunion.

_____

_____

_____

Respond—*What Will You Do with What You Know?*

(1) Read 1 Samuel 24:1–7. Based upon David's refusal to harm King Saul who wanted him dead, what lessons may be drawn regarding your response to those with whom you disagree?

_____

_____

(2) Has disagreement caused bitterness and separation in a friendship and/or division in the church?

_____

(3) Looking back at the disagreement, what common ground could possibly have resolved the issue?

_____

(4) In times of disagreement, ask the Holy Spirit, "How can I win without bruising?"[15]

(5) What is the first step you must take in reconciliation with your brother? (Matthew 5:24)

_____

---

[15] Lincoln, "Winning without Bruising?"

7

Wounded by Bereavement

"The LORD is my strength and my shield; my heart trusted in him, and I am helped: therefore my heart greatly rejoiceth; and with my song will I praise him" (Psalm 28:7). C. S. Lewis declared, "Christians never say good-bye!"[16] Warren Wiersbe stated "God's people live by promises, not by explanations."[17]

Review—*Truths the Chapter Taught*

(1) Billy Graham said that when a loved one dies, our grief is not a sign of weak faith but of great

_____

(2) Encapsulate the definition of grief as cited by the following men.

C. S. Lewis _____

J. I Packer _____

Jay Adams _____

(3) The Greek word for grace is *charis*. What does it mean? _____

_____

(4) Explain the meaning of death and its process, according to Max Anders.

_____

_____

_____

(5) C. H. Spurgeon explained the use of the term "soul sleep" in Scripture. Summarize the explanation.

_____

_____

---

[16] Jones, 77.

[17] Morgan, 767.

(6) An essential in grief recovery is staying connected to God. How is that achieved?

_____

_____

(7) Describe the benefit of "tears" in the grief experience? _____

_____

(8) Cite four Bible verses which may be personalized and used as prayers.

_____

(9) What is the value of singing in your grief? _____

_____

Reflect—*Consider What This Means*

(1) Paul said, "For now we see through a glass, darkly; but then face to face: now I know in part; but then shall I know even as also I am known" (1 Corinthians 13:12). What hope does this text give the bereaved? (see John 20:16; Matthew 17:1–4) _____

_____

(2) "Worry is a thin stream of fear trickling through our minds; if encouraged, it cuts a channel into which all other thoughts are drained." Give your reflection of the meaning of that statement. _____

_____

_____

(3) Solomon says, "A cheerful heart is good medicine, but a broken spirit saps a person's strength" (Proverbs 17:22, NLT). What is the value of laughter in the grief experience? _____

_____

_____

(4) Describe the importance of involving others in your grief. _____

Wounded by Bereavement

Respond—*What Will You Do with What You Know?*

(1) Of the definitions cited in the *Review—Truths the Chapter Taught,* which one ministers most to you, and why? _____

_____

(2) How important is it to articulate your grief? _____

_____

(3) C. S. Lewis, writing of the death of his wife, said, "How wicked it would be, if we could, to call the dead back! She said not to me but to the chaplain, 'I am at peace with God.'"[18] Do you agree with Lewis, and if so, why?

_____

_____

(4) What happens when someone tries to recapture the past, according to Billy Graham? _____

_____

(5) Read Galatians 6:2. What benefit is derived from ministering to others while yet hurting? _____

(6) Describe the horrendous pain due to grief you are experiencing and what you are doing to find comfort, strength and hope to press on? _____

_____

_____

_____

(7) To whom can you minister this week who is walking the path of sorrow that you are walking? _____

(8) Remember, accepting your loved ones' deaths is not forgetting them.

_____

[18] Lewis.

8

Wounded by Discouraging Remarks

"Therefore, my beloved brethren, be ye stedfast, unmoveable, always abounding in the work of the Lord, forasmuch as ye know that your labour is not in vain in the Lord" (1 Corinthians 15:58). Alan Redpath said, "For every discouragement has been allowed to come to us in order that through it we may be cast in utter helplessness at the Savior's feet."[19]

Review—*Truths the Chapter Taught*

(1) According to Alan Redpath, what is the major purpose of discouragement? _____

_____

(2) John Calvin cautions us not to _____

_____

(3) What do the following Scriptures teach about our response to discouragement?

Romans 8:26 _____

2 Corinthians 12:9 _____

Psalm 31:24 _____

Proverbs 13:6 _____

(4) In what way did Judah endeavor to discourage Nehemiah from continuation of the work of rebuilding the walls about Jerusalem? (Nehemiah 4:10)

_____

_____

(5) What was Nehemiah's response to Judah? (Nehemiah 4:20) _____

_____

---

[19] http://christian-quotes.ochristian.com/Discouragement-Quotes.

(6) Sanballat also sought to discourage the work of Nehemiah from being accomplished in seven ways. List these seven ways that discouragement confronts the believer.

Slander

_____

_____

Lies

_____

_____

Ridicule

(7) Describe the discouragement David had to surmount to conquer Goliath.

From his brothers _____

From King Saul _____

(8) What was David's response?

To his brothers (1 Samuel 17:29) _____

To King Saul (1 Samuel 17:34–37) _____

(9) David won the battle with Goliath due to utilizing four principles. Summarize each following its listing.

Think Big _____

Talk Big _____

Believe Big _____

Do Big _____

Reflect—*Consider What This Means*

(1) David declared, "The LORD hath prepared his throne in the heavens; and his kingdom ruleth over all" (Psalm 103:19). What is David declaring about God's sovereign control of everything, and how does that relate to your present circumstance? _____

_____

_____

Wounded by Discouraging Remarks

(2) Hudson Taylor said, "All giants have been weak men and women who did great things for God because they reckoned on His power and presence to be with them."[20] What positive push do you derive from Taylor's words to press forward despite discouraging remarks?

_____

_____

(3) You are not to discount the counsel of the godly with regard to God's call to a specific work. What do the following Scriptures state about godly counsel?

Proverbs 15:22 _____

Proverbs 11:14 _____

Proverbs 1:5 _____

Proverbs 12:15 _____

(4) Seriously weigh the counsel of the godly but ultimately rely upon the Holy Spirit to give guidance.

Respond—*What Will You Do with What You Know?*

(1) At any point in life, has someone sought to discourage you from doing that which was the will of the Lord? _____

When: _____

How: _____

_____

_____

Result: _____

_____

(2) Apply Nehemiah's five keys to success to your life.

Focus _____

Faith _____

---

[20] Zuck, 169.

Fight (prayer) _____

Fortitude _____

Finish _____

(3) How might discouragement be used for good by God in your life? (Romans 8:28) _____

_____

(4) What godly counsel would you give someone who is being told he does not have what it takes to succeed in that which is the plan of God?

_____

_____

_____

(5) Paul declares, "Therefore, my beloved brethren, be ye stedfast, unmoveable, always abounding in the work of the Lord, forasmuch as ye know that your labour is not in vain in the Lord" (1 Corinthians 15:58). Relate this verse to your present struggle and detail what it says to you personally.

_____

_____

_____

9

Wounded by Belittlement

"Do not use harmful words, but only helpful words, the kind that build up and provide what is needed, so that what you say will do good to those who hear you" (Ephesians 4:29, GNT). All bitterness or anger toward the person who belittled you must be released unto the Lord in confessional prayer. Ever determine not to do unto others what they did unto you.

Review—*Truths the Chapter Taught*

(1) The two types of people who impact our lives are _____ people and _____ people.

(2) Describe the basement person. _____
_____
_____

(3) Describe the balcony person. _____
_____
_____

(4) What is meant by the term "positive push"? _____
_____

(5) Share four definitions of the role of an encourager.

"to fill with courage or strength of purpose"

_____
_____
_____

Reflect—*Consider What This Means*

(1) In what ways was Barnabas a balcony person to:

Paul _____

John Mark _____

(2) Derek Redmond in the 1992 Barcelona Olympics was in the middle of his heat when he fell to the ground. In what ways was his father a balcony person at that time to him? _____

_____

(3) Encapsulate in one or two sentences the role of an encourager based on the four definitions shared in the *Review—Truths the Chapter Taught.*

_____

_____

(4) Give your reflection on the teaching in Ephesians 4:29._____

_____

_____

Respond—*What Will You Do with What You Know?*

(1) Have you experienced a "positive push" that encouraged you to accomplish a certain task? _____

(2) Share your story regarding a "positive push." _____

_____

_____

_____

(3) Look for opportunities this week to be a balcony person to another and give him a "positive push."

(4) Of the four most powerful words that may be spoken, which have been said to you? _____

What impact did they have upon your life?

_____

With whom might you share them this week? _____

(5) Who has played the greater role as a balcony person in your life?

_____

Wounded by Belittlement

Today write him a letter or send a card expressing gratitude. Ponder where you might be had that person not allowed God to use him in this manner.

(6) If you embrace bitterness or anger toward the person who belittled you, release it unto the Lord in confessional prayer.

10

Wounded by Rejection

"He [Jesus] came unto his own, and his own received him not" (John 1:11). The denial of love and acceptance in our lives by people who matter wounds, crushes our spirit. Their rejection infuses feelings of unworthiness, hopelessness, shame, and despair. Nothing, not even the grief of death, compares to the anguish and pain in hearing the horrendous message repeatedly, "You don't measure up to our standards. You are unwanted and unwelcome."

Review—*Truths the Chapter Taught*

(1) Describe Jesus' rejection. _____

_____

(2) C. H. Spurgeon explains the meaning of *acceptance* in Ephesians 1:6. Summarize that explanation. _____

_____

_____

(3) King Saul is a classic example of reacting to rejection wrongly (1 Samuel 18:7–11). Why? _____

_____

(4) In what ways does rejection breed a rejection complex? _____

_____

Reflect—*Consider What This Means*

(1) Reflect upon the statement, "Don't read into the rejection things not there." _____

_____

(2) Read Romans 8:28. How might God bring good out of your rejection encounter? _____

(3) John 10:10 tells of the purpose of Satan in your life. In what ways do you believe Satan seeks to destroy your life (happiness, purpose, self-worth, hope)? _____

_____

How can you stop him? _____

(4) In what ways have you allowed rejection to influence your life? _____

_____

_____

(5) Contrast the difference between *rational* and *irrational* beliefs and how they impact one's identity.

Irrational Belief	Rational Belief
_____	_____
_____	_____
_____	_____
_____	_____
_____	_____

Respond—*What Will You Do with What You Know?*

(1) Tell your story of being told "I have no room for you." _____

_____

(2) Stated in Scripture are numerous texts that refer to who you are in Christ Jesus. Select five of these texts and detail what they state about your identity in Christ Jesus.

_____

_____

_____

_____

_____

Take a few moments to thank God for this lofty and exalted position in His kingdom.

(3) What does God want you to learn from the rejection experience?

_____

Wounded by Rejection

(4) Is it possible that your perception of rejection at times was wrong? Explain your answer.

_____

_____

(5) Do you let others define who you are (parents, friends, classmates, coaches, teachers) or the Word of God? _____

(6) Whom do you need to forgive for the hurt caused by their rejection?

_____

Ask God for added grace to exhibit forgiveness.

11

Wounded by a Child's Scorn

"Honour thy father and thy mother: that thy days may be long upon the land which the LORD thy God giveth thee" (Exodus 20:12). Charles Stanley advises, "Don't make your acceptance [of your children] contingent upon their appearance, personality, or performance. Shower genuine affection on your kids, and they will do their best to please you."[21]

Review—*Truths the Chapter Taught*

(1) What is the prophecy recorded in Matthew 10:21? _____

_____

(2) Who should take the initiative in reconciliation between parents and children? _____

Why? _____

(3) Share some possible approaches as a parent to a rebellious child. ____

_____

_____

(4) Shakespeare said, "How sharper than a serpent's tooth it is to have a thankless child."[22] In what ways are children "thankless"? _____

_____

(5) Are you a "thankless child"; and, if so, in what ways? _____

_____

_____

Reflect—*Consider What This Means*

(1) Harriet Beecher Stowe (1811–1896), author of *Uncle Tom's Cabin,* said, "The bitterest tears shed over graves are for words left unsaid and deeds left

---

[21] Stanley, "Training Our Children."

[22] Shakespeare.

~ 41 ~

undone." Upon the sudden death of your parent or child, what is it that you would regret not having said or done? _____

_____

(2) As a child who is at odds with his parents, reflect upon the lesson taught in the story of the "yellow ribbons" tied to the limbs of an old oak tree.

_____

_____

(3) Forgiveness is not to be based upon your children's or parents' forgiveness of you. You are to forgive whether they exhibit forgiveness or not. Pause now, asking the Lord to forgive you for withholding forgiveness from your child/parent. Plan this week to personally contact your child/parent requesting his or her forgiveness.

Respond—*What Will You Do with What You Know?*

(1) The answer shared in the *Reflect—Consider What This Means* section regarding regrets (question 1) should be acted upon immediately. Determine to make that contact, do that deed, say that word this week.

(2) What lesson do you derive from the story of the rebellious son who was told to shoot his mother? _____

_____

_____

(3) Spend time in praying for your wayward child or for the parent from which you are estranged.

12

Wounded by Sexual Abuse

"To appoint unto them that mourn in Zion, to give unto them beauty for ashes, the oil of joy for mourning, the garment of praise for the spirit of heaviness; that they might be called trees of righteousness, the planting of the LORD, that he might be glorified" (Isaiah 61:3). "Sexual abuse stands as one of the most devastating sins that human beings have devised," states Chuck Swindoll, "leaving deep scars and unspeakable pain. Victims of sexual abuse have had much taken from them; Jesus Christ and His church have much to offer in response.[23]

Review—*Truths the Chapter Taught*

(1) What was Amnon's great sin and crime against Tamar? _____

(2) Describe what happened after the sin to Tamar. (2 Samuel 13:18–19)

_____

_____

(3) In what way was Jonadab a co-conspirator in Tamar's rape? _____

_____

(4) What is the symbolism of "torn your robe" in 2 Samuel 13:18–19? ___

_____

(5) Tamar put ashes upon her head.

What does that mean? _____

What does Jesus say He will do for such people (Isaiah 61:3)?

_____

(6) Summarize C. H. Spurgeon's statement about Isaiah 61:3.

_____

_____

_____

---

[23] Swindoll, "Sexual Abuse."

The Wounded Spirit Workbook

Reflect—*Consider What This Means*

(1) Contrast how Amnon treated Tamar after the abuse with how the community of believers should treat such a wounded person. _____

_____

(2) Why do you think David failed Tamar in giving support? _____

_____

(3) Do you agree with the author that victims of sexual abuse are still counted virgins before God? Why or why not? _____

_____

Respond—*What Will You Do with What You Know?*

(1) What was stated in the lesson that especially helped minister to your wounded spirit? _____

(2) What message does Psalm 35:14 bear for you (or someone you know that has suffered abuse)? _____

_____

(3) Sex offenders don't deserve forgiveness, but they are nonetheless to be forgiven. Are you at the point where you can, with God's strength, forgive the person that hurt you? _____

(4) If called upon to counsel another who has suffered sexual abuse, what might you advise? _____

_____

_____

13

Wounded by Unjust or Incorrect Reproof

"As an earring of gold, and an ornament of fine gold, so is a wise reprover upon an obedient ear" (Proverbs 25:12). Often the right thing is stated in the wrong manner, resulting in spirit wounding due to either ego, anger or ignorance of how it is to be handled. Much heart wounding and its intensity would be lessened if Christians would exact reproof biblically.

Review—*Truths the Chapter Taught*

(1) What is the dual objective of reproof? _____

_____

(2) What is the essential trait for the one who issues reproof? _____

_____

(3) What key elements in reproof are cited in Matthew 18:15? _____

_____

_____

(4) Eight helps for the wounded spirit due to incorrect reproof are cited. List them.

_____

_____

_____

_____

_____

_____

_____

_____

Reflect—*Consider What This Means*

(1) Summarize John Gill's picture of biblical reproof. _____

_____

_____

_____

(2) Comment on this statement: To have your actions misjudged by Christian brothers/sisters and to be on the end of sharp, compassionless and unjust rebuke because of it is exceedingly painful. _____

_____

_____

Respond—*What Will You Do with What You Know?*

(1) Describe your experience with reproof, indicating whether or not it followed biblical guidelines. _____

_____

_____

(2) What was your response to the reproof? _____

_____

_____

(3) In the *Review—Truths the Chapter Taught,* you cited eight helps for the wounded spirit due to incorrect reproof. What additional help(s) would you add to the list? _____

_____

_____

(4) How might you help someone who was wounded by incorrect or unjust reproof?

_____

_____

(5) To whom have you played the role of a sincere but wrong Bildad?

_____

This week make an earnest attempt to acknowledge your wrong with the person.

14

Wounded by Hypocrisy

"Be kind and compassionate to one another, forgiving each other, just as in Christ God forgave you" (Ephesians 4:32, NIV). Adrian Rogers said, "Expect there to be hypocrites in the Church. The Devil is at work and every church has them."[24]

Review—*Truths the Chapter Taught*

(1) What often happens to a person who is wounded due to the hypocrisy of a spiritual leader?

_____

_____

(2) Explain the meaning of 1 Timothy 5:19. _____

_____

_____

(3) In what ways did the following spiritual leaders falter?

     Peter: _____

     Barnabas: _____

     Euodias and Syntyche: _____

     Demas: _____

(4) In responding to hypocrisy, seek to be redemptive (restorative) instead of _____.

(5) In the event you depart the church due to a leader's hypocrisy, must you still exhibit forgiveness toward him/her? (Ephesians 4:32) _____

     Why? _____

Reflect—*Consider What This Means*

(1) "How seldom," states Thomas à Kempis "we weigh our neighbors in the same balance as ourselves."[25] What is your take on this statement?

_____

---

[24] Rogers, "Hypocrites in the Church."

[25] http://www.quotegarden.com/hypocrisy.html.

_____

(2) Ponder Romans 14:12–13. Share what the text teaches about personal accountability. _____

_____

(3) What is the lesson taught in Matthew 5:7 by Jesus? _____

_____

Respond—*What Will You Do with What You Know?*

(1) How are John Bradford's words applicable to those wounded by hypocrisy? _____

_____

(2) How would you like to be treated if you were in the shoes of the "hypocrite"? _____

_____

(3) How has your spirit been wounded due to hypocrisy, and what impact did it bear? (Withhold referencing leaders by name if this is to be shared within a group) _____

_____

_____

_____

(4) Forgive the fallen leader. Pray for healing in both the fallen one and yourself. Spend time doing both now.

15

Wounded by Sin

"He will turn again, he will have compassion upon us; he will subdue our iniquities; and thou wilt cast all their sins into the depths of the sea" (Micah 7:19). David's heart was wounded by personal sin (2 Samuel 11:4). He testifies, "My guilt overwhelms me—it is a burden too heavy to bear. My wounds fester and stink because of my foolish sins. I am bent over and racked with pain. All day long I walk around filled with grief" (Psalm 38:4–6, NLT). David goes on to say that even friends abandoned him (v. 11), which surely intensified the grief.

All have experienced failure in their spiritual walk and identify with David's pain.

Review—*Truths the Chapter Taught*

(1) Summarize Oswald Chambers' statement about what we are to do with the broken and irreversible things of the past. _____

_____

_____

(2) "Can it be possible that sin, such sin as mine, can be forgiven, forgiven altogether and forever?"[26] How does C. H. Spurgeon answer the question?

_____

_____

_____

(3) Describe how David's spirit was wounded due to personal sin? (Psalm 38:4–6, 11) _____

_____

_____

(4) In Scripture, one finds a long list of those who failed besides David. Name three of these and how they failed.

_____

_____

---

[26] Spurgeon, *Morning and Evening,* November 27.

_____

_____

(5) Write a brief narrative regarding the sin of Samson (Judges 16). _____

_____

_____

_____

_____

(6) In Matthew 18:22, Jesus teaches what truth about "second-chances"?

_____

Reflect—*Consider What This Means*

(1) All who visit the Devil's barber shop through engaging in pornography, drugs and alcohol usage, sexual immorality, dishonesty, etc., will have clipped from their life what was clipped from Samson's. What four things were "clipped" from Samson's life by the enemy of the soul?

_____

_____

_____

_____

(2) Describe each step in the pathway to forgiveness and healing of the wounded spirit due to sin?

Recognize it. _____

Repent of it. _____

Release it. _____

Rebound from it. _____

(3) A young man asked a veterinarian, "If a bird breaks its wing, will it ever be able to soar as high as it once did?" The veterinarian replied, "It all depends on who mends its wing." Have you ever broken a "wing" and had it completely mended by the Lord? Do you know of others who have? Knowledge of such

~ 50 ~

Wounded by Sin

should give assurance that God is both willing and able to do it again for you and others.

(4) How did Martin Luther respond to the accusatory attacks of Satan regarding past sin? _____

Determine to respond accordingly when Satan drags up before you sins of the past that are under the blood and totally forgiven by God.

(5) What spiritual lesson does the Rose Bowl blunder by Roy teach about God's graciousness to give man second chances?

_____

_____

Respond—*What Will You Do with What You Know?*

(1) Are you a Samson? Outwardly you cast the portrayal of happiness while inwardly the torment of past sin is ripping you apart. Has the peace of God that passes all understanding been replaced with guilt, fear, shame, and despair?

_____

(2) Relate your wounded spirit to that of David's. (Psalm 38:4–6, 11)

_____

_____

_____

(3) How much encouragement regarding God's complete forgiveness of sin does Hebrews 11:32 afford your heart? _____

_____

(4) C. H. Spurgeon said, "Sins of all kinds He treats as if they had never been, as if they were quite erased from His memory. Oh, miracle of grace!"[27] Ponder the biblical foundation for this statement and then lay your sin at His feet in godly sorrow, asking forgiveness and restoration. (1 John 1:7–9)

(5) What are your thoughts about Corrie ten Boom's statement about forgiveness? _____

---

[27] Ibid, July 23.

16

Wounded by Spiritual Warfare

"And they overcame him by the blood of the Lamb, and by the word of their testimony; and they loved not their lives unto the death" (Revelation 12:11). "There is an adversary," writes E. Y. Mullins, "whose intelligence so far surpasses yours that it cannot be mentioned in comparison, whose power transcends yours so far that they ought never to be placed side by side, who has the experience of six thousand years of conflict, who has been in direct and personal conflict with God Himself, who has placed his foot upon the hearts of ten thousand foes, who has brought to naught the physical strength of Samson, the intellectual culture of Solomon, the piety of David, and millions of men and women—the Devil."[28]

Review—*Truths the Chapter Taught*

(1) What is Satan's threefold purpose cited in John 10:10?

_____

_____

_____

(2) Why would Satan attack your mind? _____

_____

(3) Satan's accusations are responsible for what in the believer's life?

_____

(4) Explain the meaning of 1 John 2:1–2. _____

_____

(5) Define each piece of the believer's armor.

The Belt of Truth. _____

The Breastplate of Righteousness. _____

The Gospel Shoes. _____

The Shield of Faith. _____

---

[28] Matthews, 42.

The Helmet of Salvation. _____

The Sword of the Spirit. _____

The Knees of Prayer. _____

(6) Martyn Lloyd-Jones states it is imperative to put on all the armor. Why? _____

(7) How is the armor to be put on? _____

Reflect—*Consider What This Means*

(1) Relate the story of the harassed apartment tenet to that of the believer and Satan. _____

_____

(2) Why is the name of Jesus the believer's power word? (Philippians 2:9–11) _____

(3) What impressions did you receive regarding the story of missionary E. P. Scott? _____

_____

(4) How might you use the name of Jesus in battling Satan? _____

_____

_____

Respond—*What Will You Do with What You Know?*

(1) A. W. Tozer encourages the believer to talk back to the Devil when harassed. Write out what you might say to Satan when he accuses you of sin that long has been forgiven.

_____

_____

(2) In what ways may you obey Ephesians 4:27?

_____

_____

Wounded by Spiritual Warfare

(3) What is Kingdom authority, and how does it relate to you when battling Satan?

_____

_____

(4) How might you differentiate between Satan's accusations and the Holy Spirit's conviction?

_____

_____

(5) What weapon did Jesus use in defeating Satan in the wilderness?

_____

What does this say regarding the place and power of the Word of God in battling Satan? _____

(6) What role does prayer play in battling Satan? (Luke 18:1) _____

_____

17

Wounded by Divorce

"There is therefore now no condemnation to them which are in Christ Jesus" (Romans 8:1). Just because the divorce papers are signed doesn't mean the ordeal is over. It isn't. The emotional trauma of divorce which includes anger, fear, rejection, bitterness, anxiety, and loneliness yet has to be addressed, or else it will impact life permanently. Sadly, many who have been divorced for years are yet bearing the wound of divorce due to its improper handling when it happened.

Review—*Truths the Chapter Taught*

(1) What is Adrian Rogers' view of divorce? _____

_____

_____

(2) Does separation equal divorce? Why or why not? _____

_____

_____

(3) Psychologist Thomas Whiteman states there are six stages of divorce recovery. Describe each stage briefly.

        Denial: _____

        Anger: _____

        Bargaining: _____

        Depression: _____

        Acceptance: _____

        Forgiveness: _____

(4) In the healing process, it's important for two reasons that personal faults that contributed to the break-up be identified. What are they?

_____

_____

Reflect—*Consider What This Means*

(1) You are to forgive your former spouse. Complete this statement: You don't forgive them because they deserve forgiveness but because _____

_____

(2) Reflect on Romans 8:28 and share how it applies to divorce. _____

_____

(3) Read again "What I need from my mom and dad: A child's list of wants." Are you taking into serious consideration the hurt and needs of your child (children)? What should be done to assure they will not be wounded profoundly by the divorce? _____

_____

_____

_____

(4) Susan Pease Gadoua states, "I liken the undoing of a marriage to trying to disentangle two trees that have grown next to each other for years. The more intertwined the root systems are, the longer it will take for the trees to go their separate ways."[29] Based on Gadoua's statement, what might you anticipate occurring upon divorce? _____

_____

(5) Christopher Columbus said, "You can never cross the ocean unless you have the courage to lose sight of the shore." How does this statement apply to divorce? _____

_____

(6) Are there any legitimate grounds sanctioned by Scripture for divorce? (Matthew 19:9; 1 Corinthians 7:13–16; Mark 10:11–12) If so, what are they?

_____

_____

---

[29] Gadoua.

Wounded by Divorce

Respond—*What Will You Do with What You Know?*

(1) How important is it to accept the fact of divorce once it has occurred?

_____

_____

(2) Do you exhibit anger toward the former spouse? How might it be resolved? _____

_____

(3) As a divorced person (or one who knows divorcees), do you perceive that many in the church think divorcees are "second-class" citizens or church members? Why or why not? _____

_____

_____

(4) In the healing process, it is important to receive the forgiveness of God, verbalize the hurt with friends, and free yourself from things that trigger painful memories. Another healing medicine is to set boundaries. What boundaries do you need to set? _____

_____

(5) What advice would you give a child of divorce who has been wounded deeply? _____

_____

18

Wounded by Unforgiveness

"Then came Peter to him, and said, Lord, how oft shall my brother sin against me, and I forgive him? till seven times? Jesus saith unto him, I say not unto thee, Until seven times: but, Until seventy times seven" (Matthew 18:21–22). Charles Stanley states, "We are to forgive so that we may enjoy God's goodness without feeling the weight of anger burning deep within our hearts. Forgiveness does not mean we recant the fact that what happened to us was wrong. Instead, we roll our burdens onto the Lord and allow Him to carry them for us."[30]

Review—*Truths the Chapter Taught*

(1) C. S. Lewis said, "To be a Christian means to forgive the inexcusable, because _____

(2) What is the definition of forgiveness from the following persons?

Corrie ten Boom _____

_____

Jon Courson _____

_____

John MacArthur _____

_____

(3) What did John MacArthur state regarding the promise of God in Romans 8:28? _____

_____

(4) What is the lesson of Ezekiel 3:15 with regard to the hurt experienced at the hands of another? _____

_____

(5) In what way is forgiveness costly to both God and you?

You. _____

_____

---

[30] Stanley, *Landmines in the Path of the Believer.*

God. _____

_____

(6) William Barclay said, "Where there is forgiveness, someone must be crucified (that is, self)."[31] What do you think Barclay meant by the statement?

_____

Have you ever "crucified" yourself to forgive another? _____

(7) What is the teaching of Jesus about forgiveness in Matthew 18:21?

_____

(8) Describe the seven consequences of unforgiveness.

Long-term illnesses (possible, not always) _____

Grave emotional problems _____

Mean disposition _____

Control by the flesh _____

Hindrance to relationships _____

Forfeiture of peace _____

Broken fellowship with God _____

Reflect—*Consider What This Means*

(1) Do you agree with the following statement by John MacArthur, and if so, state why? "That means unforgivingness is no less an offense to God than fornication or drunkenness, even though it is sometimes deemed more acceptable."[32] _____

_____

(2) How should Christians respond to those who hurt them?

1 Peter 3:9 _____

Romans 12:17–21 _____

_____

[31] Barclay, *Letter to the Hebrews,* 108.

[32] MacArthur, 97.

Wounded by Unforgiveness

(3) God commands that we bless those who do us injury. How can you do that? _____

_____

(4) What is the lesson of the boy who sat on a bumble bee? _____

_____

(5) Explain the meaning of Proverbs 10:12. _____

_____

(6) Is it always necessary to confront the person who offended you? Why or why not? _____

_____

_____

(7) Explain the meaning of Matthew 18:15. _____

_____

(8) Complete the following sentences regarding misconceptions about forgiveness.

Forgiveness is synonymous with _____

Forgiveness always means resumption of the close _____

Forgiveness is allowing the _____ to continue.

Forgiveness is an _____ "fuzzy feeling."

Forgiveness banishes immediately the _____ caused by the offender.

Forgiveness has its _____.

Forgiveness is to be extended based on the offender's expression of _____ and _____.

Forgiveness is synonymous with making an _____.

(9) What does the story of Joseph's ill treatment by his brothers teach regarding the outcome of personal hurt? (Genesis 50:20) _____

_____

List some benefits derived from being injured by another. _____

_____

(10) Describe the difference between making an apology and asking for-giveness. _____

Respond—*What Will You Do with What You Know?*

(1) Respond to this statement: "He doesn't deserve my forgiveness; there-fore, I am justified in not forgiving him. _____

_____

_____

(2) It's easy to gossip about and belittle the person who has wounded your spirit instead of confronting him personally. Such behavior, in addition to being sinful, is cowardly. Brazen up and talk directly to that person this week.

(3) How might lowering expectations from others prevent personal hurt?

_____

_____

(4) Comment on the statement "Forgiving is not an erasure." _____

_____

_____

(5) What is the severity of your wound caused by another in comparison to the atrocities Corrie ten Boom experienced? _____

_____

(6) Comment on the statement "The epitome of hypocrisy is the claim to love God while withholding love from others."[33] _____

_____

(7) Take some time to Meditate upon and then pray Andrew Murray's prayer on forgiveness

.

---

[33] King James Version Study Bible, 1 John 4:19.

(8) Determine this week to confront the person who hurt you with meekness, requesting forgiveness (if the offense calls for it); otherwise, forgive him and move on with your life. "To forgive is to set a prisoner free and discover that the prisoner was you."[34]

---

[34] http://www.brainyquote.com/quotes/authors/l/lewis_b_smedes.html.

19

Wounded by Guilt and Shame

"Make me to hear joy and gladness; that the bones which thou hast broken may rejoice" (Psalm 51:8). Upon doing wrong, with godly repentance you confessed it to God and were forgiven. Then why still the heart-crushing, soul-accusing guilt? Why the humiliating shame? The bottom line is that guilt and shame are Satan's insidious robbers of our happiness, peace of mind and self-worth which are spurred by him continuously in the heart. Jesus said, "The thief cometh not, but for to steal, and to kill, and to destroy: I am come that they might have life, and that they might have it more abundantly" (John 10:10).

Review—*Truths the Chapter Taught*

(1) There are two kinds of guilt mentioned in the Bible. Name and describe them. _____

_____

(2) The key to victory over haunting, hurting guilt is in recognizing its source (Satan, the father of lies) and steadfastly, stoutly rejecting any place to it (John 8:44)

(3) Far too many Christians are in bondage to _____.

(4) The stronghold of false, unhealthy guilt is torn down by _____.

(5) Explain the meaning of Colossians 2:13–14. _____

_____

Reflect—*Consider What This Means*

(1) Meditate upon Isaiah 43:25. What does this text mean to you?

_____

_____

(2) Encapsulate the promise of the forgiveness of God in the following texts.

John 1:29 _____

Hebrews 10:17 _____

Isaiah 1:17–18 _____

Isaiah 44:22 _____

Isaiah 55:7 _____

Micah 7:19 _____

Psalm 103:12 _____

(3) How does the Old Testament scapegoat express the New Testament atonement provided by Jesus? _____

_____

(4) Describe the six steps to freedom from guilt.

_____

_____

_____

_____

_____

_____

Respond—*What Will You Do with What You Know?*

(1) "Why do we claim on one hand our sins are gone and on the other act just as though they are not gone?"[35] _____

_____

_____

(2) Comment on the statement by C. H. Spurgeon on the Christian's permanent acceptance in God. _____

_____

_____

(3) What is meant by "double jeopardy" with regard to sin? _____

_____

---

[35] Tozer, 12–13.

Wounded by Guilt and Shame

(4) Are you guilty of "double jeopardy"? _____

(5) Which steps to freedom from guilt over sin God has long since forgiven do you yet need to take? _____

_____

20

Wounded by Bullying

"God will bless you when people insult you, mistreat you, and tell all kinds of evil lies about you because of me" (Matthew 5:11, CEV). Bill Mayer states, "The emotional scars that result from bullying can last a lifetime. Children who have been bullied may sink into patterns of antisocial behavior such as vandalism or even look to drugs and alcohol as sources of relief. Constant bullying in school can interfere with a child's education and mental and physical health."[36]

Review—*Truths the Chapter Taught*

(1) There is an apparent connection between bullying or being bullied, and _____.

(2) Every _____ is a mad rush to end "unbearable pain" without thought to its ultimate end of permanent separation from family and friends.

(3) Jesus identifies the real source of bullying in John 10:10. Identify the source. _____

(4) Why is it important to keep a record/journal of bullying encounters?

_____

(5) List some possible telltale signs of bullying in the workplace.

_____

_____

(6) What action in the workplace may be taken to counter bullying?

_____

_____

(7) When is intervention by parents and/or school officials warranted with regard to bullying? _____

(8) How is *telling* on a bully actually helping the bully? _____

_____

---

[36] Mayer, 8.

Reflect—*Consider What This Means*

(1) What is the meaning of the illustration of the twenty-dollar bill? _____

_____

(2) What is the spiritual lesson of the "checkmate" illustration? _____

_____

(3) How might bullying be prevented? _____

_____

(4) What is meant by the statement, "Don't let the bully see you ruffled"?

_____

_____

(5) The bullies obviously have problems with jealousy, self-esteem, acceptance, or attention. Pray that God will meet them at their point of deepest need.

Respond—*What Will You Do with What You Know?*

(1) "Humpty Dumpty sat on a wall; Humpty Dumpty had a great fall. All the king's horses and all the king's men couldn't put Humpty together again." Do you feel like Humpty Dumpty? In what ways? _____

_____

_____

(2) In the classic poem "The Land of Beginning Again," the writer longs for a land where she can lay aside the past, much as a man puts aside soiled clothes to start fresh. Although in the poem this "Land of Beginning Again" is make-believe, for Christians there is such a place found in a personal relationship with Jesus Christ. The Bible calls the refreshing new beginning "the new birth." If you have not experienced the new birth, "The Land of Beginning Again," receive Jesus into your life now.

(3) Are you a victim of religious bullying? Comment on the teaching of Jesus with regard to such in Matthew 5:10. _____

_____

In Scripture, who was a victim of religious bullying? _____

_____

Wounded by Bullying

_____

(4) Apply the story of the young violinist to your life. _____

_____

_____

(5) When bullied, are you prone to believe that you are responsible for it? Why or why not? _____

(6) What action will you take with regard to school place or workplace bullying (either for yourself or another)? _____

_____

21
Wounded by Failure

"Then came the disciples to Jesus apart, and said, Why could not we cast him [demon] out?" (Matthew 17:19). The disciples experienced failure in ministry; all do at some point. The key is how we respond to the failure.

Review—*Truths the Chapter Taught*

(1) What is the lesson of the little boy with the baseball cap? _____

_____

(2) Failure doesn't mean the task isn't to be done by you. Why? _____

_____

(3) How might failure be viewed as a "divine detour"? _____

_____

(4) What means did God use to close one door only to open another for Elijah? (1 Kings 17:2–9) _____

_____

(5) What was Paul's encounter with "closed doors"? (Acts 16:6–10) _____

_____

(6) What is the purpose of divinely closed doors? _____

_____

(7) What did Jack London, Winston Churchill and Abraham Lincoln all have in common? _____

_____

Reflect—*Consider What This Means*

(1) What advice do Henry Blackaby and Claude King offer while waiting for the "door" to open? _____

_____

(2) Apply Psalm 27:14 to the process of waiting for an open door.

_____

_____

(3) The door did not open for Joseph quickly. He waited two years, but then it opened without a hitch. Apply Joseph's experience to your life.

Respond—*What Will You Do with What You Know?*

(1) What does Joseph's closed-door experience say about what you are experiencing presently? _____

_____

(2) Oswald Chambers gives clear counsel regarding your attitude and action when experiencing closed doors. Summarize. _____

_____

_____

(3) What happens when man tries to open a door before its time? _____

_____

(4) How can you get God's perspective of a closed door? _____

_____

22

Wounded by Loss, Sickness or Suffering

"Yea doubtless, and I count all things but loss for the excellency of the knowledge of Christ Jesus my Lord: for whom I have suffered the loss of all things, and do count them but dung, that I may win Christ" (Philippians 3:8). The bottom line is that God is with you in the dark. He has not abandoned you or "gone to sleep on the job." He will manifest Himself, grant healing, and, yes, work good out of the bad thing that happened as you wait before Him. Both the Bible and myriads of delivered saints attest to this truth.

Review—*Truths the Chapter Taught*

(1) What is the spiritual lesson of the small and stunted plant? _____

_____

(2) What spiritual lesson is taught in the story of the farmer and the bird nest? _____

_____

(3) What does it mean to "cry out" to God? _____

_____

(4) How did Joseph react to his great loss at the hands of his brothers?

_____

(5) What is the lesson regarding suffering revealed in 1 Peter 5:10? _____

_____

(6) How might Romans 8:28 minister to you in times of loss?

_____

_____

Reflect—*Consider What This Means*

(1) Meditate upon 1 Peter 5:10. What does it say, if anything, about your present circumstance? _____

_____

What promise is stated? _____

(2) What are the benefits of "crying out" to God? _____

_____

(3) A. C. Dixon said, "Reason is a servant, not a master."[37] In what ways does reason seek to be master? _____

_____

(4) Satan had to get permission from God prior to bringing great suffering and loss to Job (Job 1:12). What does this say with regard to the loss, suffering, and/or sickness you experience? _____

_____

Respond—*What Will You Do with What You Know?*

(1) Find a solitary place where unimpeded you may cry aloud to God regarding the hurt, anger, bitterness, or hatred you are experiencing with regard to personal loss with complete, unwavering confidence that He will hear and answer. (Jeremiah 33:3)

(2) Try for the next seven days "crying out" to God.

(3) What might be the lessons God wants to teach you during this time of loss? _____

_____

(4) Why was Joseph able to manifest such a loving attitude toward his brothers in his great loss? _____

_____

(5) Has God called you to the ministry of suffering? If so, for what purposes? _____

_____

_____

(6) Memorize Romans 8:28 this week.

_____

[37] Hutson, 88.

23

Wounded by Misunderstanding of Providence

"Who is among you that feareth the LORD, that obeyeth the voice of his servant, that walketh in darkness, and hath no light? let him trust in the name of the LORD, and stay upon his God" (Isaiah 50:10). Matthew Henry interprets the verse in this manner: "It is no new thing for the children and heirs of light sometimes to walk in darkness and for a time not to have any glimpse or gleam of light. This is not meant so much of the comforts of this life (those that fear God, when they have ever so great an abundance of them, do not walk in them as their light) as of their spiritual comforts, which relate to their souls. They walk in darkness when their evidences for Heaven are clouded, their joy in God is interrupted, the testimony of the Spirit is suspended, and the light of God's countenance is eclipsed."[38]

Review—*Truths the Chapter Taught*

(1) What type of darkness is Isaiah referencing in Isaiah 50:10? _____

_____

(2) List five of the reasons as to why God permits the believer to have seasons of darkness.

_____

_____

_____

_____

_____

(3) The first thing to do in darkness is _____. Why?

_____

(4) What illustration does Spurgeon use regarding the meaning of "stay upon the Lord?" _____

_____

---

[38] Matthew Henry, 1176.

The Wounded Spirit Workbook

Reflect—Consider What This Means

(1) Of the reasons stated as to why God allows seasons of darkness for the believer, which resonate the most to you? _____

_____

Why? _____

(2) What is it to "trust in the name of the Lord"? _____

_____

_____

(3) Contrast the season of darkness due to sin with that due to divine providence. _____

_____

(4) Have you been guilty of believing that all who experience darkness do so due to disobedience to God?_____ In what way has this chapter changed your view? _____

_____

Respond—What Will You Do with What You Know?

(1) Did the subject of the chapter catch you by surprise? If so, why? _____

_____

(2) Are you presently in the season of "darkness," or have you ever been? If so, describe what was experienced and why you believe God allowed it.

_____

_____

_____

_____

(3) God's name is like a strong tower. How might knowing this fact help you in the season of darkness?

_____

_____

Wounded by Misunderstanding of Providence

(4) How might you help someone in the season of darkness? _____

_____

_____

24

Lessons from the Wounded Heart

"He hath sent me to heal the brokenhearted" (Luke 4:18). C. H. Spurgeon says, "Remember Christ's *sympathy* with you. O thou who art tossed with tempest and not comforted, thy Lord's vessel is in the storm with thee! Yea, He is in the vessel with thee. There is not a pang that rends the believer's heart but He has felt it first. He drinks out of the cup with you. Is it very bitter? He has had a cup full of it for every drop that you taste. This ought to comfort you. I know of no better remedy for the heart's trouble in a Christian than to feel, 'My Master himself takes no better portion than that which He gives to me.'"[39]

Review—*Truths the Chapter Taught*

(1) It takes time for the hurt to disappear altogether. Bitterness or anger may occasionally surface, but treat them as but _____ of the ding-dongs of the bell slowing down, as described by Corrie ten Boom.

(2) Don't waste the pain, use it for gain by _____ in others what was learned when hurt, thus being a means of help and comfort.

(3) What eventually happened in the splintered relationship between John Mark and Paul? (2 Timothy 4:11) _____

_____

Does such occur in *all* relationships that are reconciled? _____

Why or why not? _____

(4) Wounded hearts need the love and concern of friends, but such that don't broach the subject of the hurt. Allow wounded hearts to pick and choose the time to dialog regarding their hurt.

(5) Encapsulate George Müller's statement on the importance of hope despite difficult circumstances. _____

_____

_____

---

[39] Spurgeon, "The Cause and Cure of a Wounded Spirit."

Reflect—*Consider What This Means*

(1) What are some triggers that recall the hurt and sorrow and need avoiding? _____

_____

(2) What is meant by taking the "high road" in dealing with the person who caused hurt? _____

_____

(3) In what ways can "uncontrolled imaginations" usurp peace and happiness? _____

_____

Share two examples.

_____

_____

(4) Summarize C. H. Spurgeon's view of Romans 8:28. _____

_____

_____

_____

(5) Kay Arthur states, "When something robs you of your peace of mind, ask yourself if it is worth the energy you are expending on it. If not, then put it out of your mind in an act of discipline. Every time the thought of 'it' returns, refuse it."[40] What is it that robs you of your peace? _____

_____

Determine today to *refuse* it by the grace of God every time the thought returns.

Respond—*What Will You Do with What You Know?*

(1) According to F. B. Meyer, what is involved in waiting upon the Lord?

_____

---

[40] *Promises and Prayers for a Dedicated Teacher*, 183.

Lessons from the Wounded Heart

(2) Comment on the statement of Oswald Chambers: "I am blind to the things which belong to my peace."[41]

_____

_____

_____

How does "spirit wounding" cause a type of spiritual blinding to that which belongs to your peace? _____

_____

How might it be resolved? _____

_____

(3) In what ways may relationships be impacted by the infliction of hurt (Paul/Barnabas)?

_____

_____

(4) List five helps from the chapter that are of greatest benefit and state why.

_____

_____

_____

_____

_____

---

[41] Chambers, April 3.

25

Healing Is Your Decision

"Come unto me, all ye that labour and are heavy laden, and I will give you rest" (Matthew 11:28). John Maxwell states, "We are either the masters or the victims of our attitudes. It is a matter of personal choice. Who we are today is the result of choices we made yesterday. Tomorrow, we will become what we choose today. To change means to choose to change."[42]

Review—*Truths the Chapter Taught*

(1) To constantly dwell on the pain of yesterday is to _____ yourself by it.

(2) Being set free from the hurt and sorrow involves five things. Name them.

Confronting of emotional issues

_____

_____

Meditation upon God's Word

_____

(3) What does hope say is the "verdict" of your present circumstance, according to R. G. Lee? _____

_____

_____

Reflect—*Consider What This Means*

(1) Apply the statement on acquiring freedom by Oswald Chambers to your present circumstance. _____

_____

_____

_____

---

[42] *Promises and Prayers for a Dedicated Teacher,* 152.

(2) John Maxwell said, "We are either the masters or the victims of our _____. It is a matter of personal choice."[43]

Respond—*What Will You Do with What You Know?*

(1) Do you want to "get well?" _____

(2) What do you need to do to get well? _____

_____

_____

_____

(3) What first "steps" can you take today to healing? _____

_____

_____

(4) Write out a prayer to God for healing.

_____

_____

_____

_____

_____

_____

_____

_____

_____

_____

_____

_____

[43] Ibid.

BIBLIOGRAPHY

Allen, Kerry James, Ed. *Exploring the Mind and Heart of the Prince of Preachers.* Oswego, IL: Fox River Press, 2005.

Barclay, William. *Letter to the Hebrews.* Louisville, KY: Westminster John Knox Press, 1967.

Barclay, W., Ed. *The Daily Study Bible Series,* The Letters of James and Peter. Philadelphia: Westminster John Knox Press, 1976.

Chambers, Oswald. *My Utmost for His Highest.*

Exell, Joseph S. *The Biblical Illustrator,* Vol. 15, Book of Acts. Grand Rapids: Baker Book House, undated.

Gadoua, Susan Pease. "How Long Does 'Typical' Divorce Recovery Take?" (April 18, 2010). http://www.psychologytoday.com, accessed August 12, 2014.

Henry, Matthew. *Matthew Henry's Commentary on the Whole Bible: Complete and Unabridged in One Volume.* Peabody: Hendrickson, 1994.

http://christian-quotes.ochristian.com, accessed April 21, 2013; July 12, 2014; June 10, 2015.

http://www.brainyquote.com/quotes/authors/l/lewis_b_smedes.html#QsYP5fSelHo XbSF5.99, accessed July 24, 2014.

http://www.quotegarden.com/hypocrisy.html, accessed July 15, 2014; August 20, 2014.

Hutson, Curtis, Ed. *Great Preaching on Comfort.* Murfreesboro, TN: Sword of the Lord Publishers, 1990.

Jones, G. C. *1000 Illustrations for Preaching and Teaching.* Nashville, TN: Broadman & Holman Publishers, 1986.

Keller, Tim. *The Wounded Spirit: Proverbs Series.* http://verticallivingministries.com/2014/01/08/tim-keller-on-the-wounded-spirit-proverbs-series, accessed March 12, 2015.

King James Version Study Bible (electronic ed.). Nashville: Thomas Nelson, 1997.

Lewis, C. S. *A Grief Observed.* cited in www.goodreads.com/work/ quotes/894384-a-grief-observed, accessed July 31, 2014.

Lincoln, Dick. "Winning without Bruising?" sermon preached September 7, 2014, Shandon Baptist Church, Columbia, SC.

MacArthur, John. *The Freedom and Power of Forgiveness,* (electronic ed.). Wheaton, IL: Crossway Books.

Matthews, C. E. *Every Christian's Job.*

Mayer, Bill, Gen. Ed. *Help, My Child is Being Bullied.* Carol Stream, Illinois: Tyndale House Publishers, 2006.

Merritt, James. "Don't Get Bitter; Get Better."

Morgan, R. J. *Nelson's Complete Book of Stories, Illustrations, and Quotes* (electronic ed.). Nashville: Thomas Nelson Publishers, 2000.

Promises and Prayers for a Cherished Friend. Brentwood, TN: Freeman-Smith, 2012.

Promises and Prayers for a Dedicated Teacher. Brentwood, TN: Freeman-Smith, 2012.

Rogers, Adrian. "The Root of Bitterness." http://www.oneplace.com/ ministries/love-worth-finding/read/articles/root-of-bitterness-8599.html, accessed July 2, 2014.

———. "Hypocrites in the Church." www.lwf.org, accessed March 6, 2015.

Shakespeare, William. *King Lear,* Act I, Scene IV, 13. nfs.sparknotes.com, accessed May 25, 2011.

Spence-Jones, H. D. M., Ed. *The Pulpit Commentary.* London; New York: Funk & Wagnalls Company, 1909.

Spurgeon. C. H. "The Cause and Cure of a Wounded Spirit," Sermon # 2494, April 16th, 1885. http://www.ccel.org, accessed December 8, 2013; September 14, 2014; September 15, 2014.

———. *Morning and Evening.*

Stanley, Charles. "Training Our Children, Proverbs 22:6." www.intouch.org, accessed February 18, 2015.

———. *Landmines in the Path of the Believer.* Nashville: Thomas Nelson, 2007.

Stott, John. Langham Partnership Daily Thought, A Service of Langham Partnership International & John Stott Ministries.

Swindoll, Chuck. "Sexual Abuse." http://www.insight.org/resources/ topics/sexual-abuse, accessed October 21, 2014.

———. *Elijah: A Man of Heroism and Humility.* Nashville: Word Publishing, 2000.

———. *Paul: A Man of Grace and Grit.* Nashville: Word Publishing, 2002.

———. *Job: A Man of Heroic Endurance.* Nashville: W Publishing Group, 2004.

Tozer, A. W. *I Talk Back to the Devil.* Harrisburg, PA: Christian Publications, Inc., 1972.

Zuck, Roy. *The Speaker's Quote Book.* Grand Rapids: Kregel Publications, 1997.

www.ingramcontent.com/pod-product-compliance
Lightning Source LLC
Chambersburg PA
CBHW060953040426
42445CB00011B/1139